KV-575-560

H.G. WELLS'S

The Truth About Pyecraft

Peter Leigh

Published in association with The Basic Skills Agency

Hodder & Stoughton

A MEMBER OF THE HODDER HEADLINE GROUP

Acknowledgements
Cover: David Hopkins
Illustrations: David Hopkins
Photograph: Hulton Getty

Every effort has been made to trace copyright holders of material reproduced in this book. Any rights not acknowledged will be acknowledged in subsequent printings if notice is given to the publisher.

Orders; please contact Bookpoint Ltd, 39 Milton Park, Abingdon, Oxon OX14 4TD. Telephone: (44) 01235 400414, Fax: (44) 01235 400454. Lines are open from 9.00–6.00, Monday to Saturday, with a 24 hour message answering service.
Email address: orders@bookpoint.co.uk

British Library Cataloguing in Publication Data
A catalogue record for this title is available from the British Library

ISBN 0 340 77465 7

First published 2000
Impression number 10 9 8 7 6 5 4 3 2 1
Year   2005 2004 2003 2002 2001 2000

Original text copyright by the Literary Executors of the Estate of H G Wells

Typeset by GreenGate Publishing Services, Tonbridge, Kent.
Printed in Great Britain for Hodder and Stoughton Educational, a division of Hodder Headline Plc, 338 Euston Road, London NW1 3BH, by Redwood Books, Trowbridge, Wilts

About the Author

H.G. Wells was born in 1866,
and died in 1946.
He was one of the most popular writers
of his day.
His writing covers a huge range,
from science fiction, to politics, to humour.

About the Story

Most of Wells' stories are very serious.
They are about science and inventions
and the effrect they have on us.

This story is much lighter.
It is sort of scientific.
It warns us to be very careful
about the words we use.

He sits not ten metres away.
If I glance over my shoulder
I can see him.

He is looking at me.
I know he is looking at me.
With that same begging look on his face.

'Don't tell on me!' he is thinking.
'Don't tell on me!'

I won't tell.
If I wanted to tell on him
I should have told long ago.
I don't tell and I don't tell,
and he ought to feel happy.
In any case who would believe me
if I did tell?

Poor old Pyecraft!
The fattest man in London.

He sits at a little table, eating.
What is he eating?
A round of hot buttered teacake!
And his eyes are on me.
Confound him! – his eyes on me!

That settles it, Pyecraft!
Since you don't trust me,
I will tell!
Right now!
I'll write it down
as you're looking at me –
the plain truth about Pyecraft,
the truth,
the whole truth,
and nothing but the truth!

Gentlemen's clubs were places to meet, drink and eat.

I first met Pyecraft in this very club.
I was a new member,
and was sitting all alone.
In came Pyecraft,
a great rolling front of chins and stomachs.
He sat down in a chair close by me,
and wheezed for a moment.

We began talking.

He asked me a bit about myself.
But he only talked about me
in order to get to himself.
And his fatness!

'I don't expect,' he said,
'you take any more exercise than I do,
or eat any less.'
'Yet,' and he smiled his little smile,
'we are different.'

And then he began to talk about his fatness.
All he did for his fatness.
All he was going to do for his fatness.
What people had told him to do for his fatness.
What others had done for their fatness.

It was stifling.
It was dumpling talk.
It made me feel swelled to hear him.

Just listening to
Pyecraft made him
feel fat.

He went on and on.
Not just then,
but every time afterwards
that I came in the club.

to wallow – to roll
around

He would come wallowing towards me,
while I had my lunch.

He seemed to be clinging to me
for some sort of reason.
There was something in his manner –
as if he saw in me
some sort of chance.

'I'd give anything to get it down,'
he would say. 'Anything!'
And he would peer at me
over his vast cheeks and pant.
Poor old Pyecraft!

One day he said,
'Medicine doesn't have all the answers,
you know.
There are other ways.'

He stopped and stared at me.

And suddenly it clicked.
I saw what he had been hinting at.
I was quite suddenly angry with him.

'Look here,' I said.
'Who told you about my grandmother's
recipes?'

'Well …'

'Every time we've met for a week,
you've hinted to me
about that little secret of mine.'

'Well,' he said,
'now the cat's out of the bag,
I'll admit it, yes …'

'Listen,' I said,
'My grandmother's recipes
are strange things.
Dangerous too.'

'But suppose –
suppose there did happen to be one.'

'The things are strange documents,' I said.
'Even the smell of them … No!'

But after going so far
Pyecraft was determined
I should go farther.
I began to think
that if I didn't agree
he would fall on me suddenly
and smother me.

I was weak, I admit it.
But I was also angry with Pyecraft.
I was inclined to say,
'Well, take the risk, then!'

That evening I took the strange,
funny smelling box out of my safe,
and turned the rustling pages over.
Some of the writing was quite unreadable.
But I found the one I was searching for.
I sat on the floor for some time looking at it.

'Look here,' I said to Pyecraft next day.
'So far as I can make it out,
this is a recipe for Loss of Weight.
I'm not absolutely sure,
but I think it's that.
And if you take my advice
you'll leave it alone.
Because, you know, my grandmother,
so far as I can gather, was a very strange lady.
See?'

'Let me try it,' said Pyecraft.

I leant back in my chair.
I tried another way.
'What in Heaven's name, Pyecraft,
do you think you'll look like
when you get thin?'

But he wouldn't listen to reason.
I made him promise
never to say another word to me
about his fatness,
whatever happened. Never!
Then I handed him that little page.

'It's nasty stuff,' I said.

'No matter,' he said, and took it.

He goggled at it.
'But … but …' he said.

He had just discovered
that it wasn't English.

'I will translate it for you,' I said,
'as well as I can.'

I did my best.
After that we didn't speak for a fortnight.
Whenever I saw him,
I frowned and waved him away.
He respected our agreement.

At the end of the fortnight
he was as fat as ever.
Then he got a word in.

'I must speak,' he said.
'It isn't fair.
There's something wrong.
It's done me no good.'

'Where's the recipe?'

He produced it carefully
from his wallet.

I ran my eye over the items.

'Was the egg bad?' I asked.

'No. Should it have been?'

'That,' I said, 'goes without saying.
When it's not clear
how good or bad a thing is
you must get the worst.
You got fresh rattlesnake poison?'

'I got a rattlesnake from the pet shop.
It cost … it cost …'

'That's your affair anyhow.
By the way, dog here probably means
wild dog.'

For a month after that
I saw Pyecraft at the club every day.
He was as fat as ever.
He didn't say anything,
but whenever he saw me
he shook his head in despair.

Telegrams were used
for quick messages.
Then one day, quite unexpectedly, his
telegram came.

A page-boy shouted my name,
and I took the telegram and opened it at once.

'For Heaven's sake come! Pyecraft.'

I got Pyecraft's address from the hall porter.
He lived in the top half of a house nearby.
I went there as soon as I finished my lunch,
and had my coffee.

His landlady answered the door.

'Mr. Pyecraft?' I said.

She said he was ill –
he hadn't been out for two days.

'He expects me,' I said.
I gave my name and she let me in.

'He said you was to come in if you came,'
she said.
Then she whispered,
'He's locked in, Sir.'

'Locked in?'

'Locked himself in yesterday morning
and hasn't let anyone in since, sir.
And all the time swearing. Oh, my!'

'What's up?'

She shook her head sadly.
'He keeps calling for food, sir.
Heavy food he wants.
I get him what I can.
Pork, pudding, sausages, new bread.
Anything like that.
He wants it left outside, if you please,
and me to go away.
He's eating, sir,
something awful.'

I went upstairs,
and rang the bell on the landing.

'He shouldn't have tried it, anyhow,'
I said to myself.

Then I could hear a funny pattering
upon the door,
like someone feeling for the handle
in the dark.

'That you, Pyecraft?' I shouted,
and banged the door.

But for a long time the door didn't open.

13

I heard the key turn.
Then Pyecraft's voice said, 'Come in.'

I turned the handle
and opened the door.
Naturally I expected to see Pyecraft.

Well, you know, he wasn't there.

I never had such a shock in my life.
There was his room, very untidy –
plates and dishes among the books and things.
There were several chairs overturned,
but there was no Pyecraft!

'It's all right, old man.
Shut the door,' he said,
and then I discovered him.

There he was, right up close to the ceiling
in the corner by the door.
It was like some one had stuck him there.
His face was anxious and angry.
He panted and waved at me.
'Shut the door,' he said.
'I don't want anyone to know.'

I shut the door,
and went and stood away from him
and stared.

'If anything gives way and you fall down,
you'll break your neck, Pyecraft.'

'I wish I could,' he wheezed.

'A man of your age
getting up to childish tricks!'

'Don't,' he said,
and looked agonised.

agonised – in pain

'How on earth,' I said,
'are you holding on up there?'

And then I realised
that he was not holding on at all.
He was floating up there,
like a great balloon filled with gas.

He tried to push himself away
from the ceiling
and to clamber down the wall to me.

'It's that recipe,' he panted, as he did so.
'Your gran …'

The picture he was holding on to
suddenly gave way,
and he flew back to the ceiling again.
The picture smashed on to the sofa.
Bump he went against the ceiling.
He tried again more carefully,
and came down by way of the mantelpiece.

It really was a most amazing sight –
that fat, red-faced man upside down
and trying to get from the ceiling to the floor.

'That recipe,' he said. 'Too successful.'

'How?'

'Loss of weight – almost complete.'

Then, of course, I understood.

'I see, Pyecraft,' I said.
'What you wanted was a cure for fatness!
But you always called it weight.
You would call it weight.'

Somehow I was extremely pleased.
I quite liked Pyecraft for the moment.

'Let me help you!' I said.
I took his hand and pulled him down.
He kicked about,
trying to get foothold somewhere.
It was like holding a flag on a windy day.

'That table,' he said,
'is solid wood and very heavy.
If you can put me under that.'

I did,
and there he wallowed about
like a captive balloon.
I stood on his hearth rug and talked to him.

Tell me,' I said, 'what happened?'

'I took it,' he said.

'How did it taste?'

'Oh, horrible!'

They all do.
I don't know whether it's the ingredients
or the results,
but all my grandmother's recipes
are very uninviting.
To me, that is.

'I took a little sip first.'

'Yes?'

'As I felt lighter and better after an hour,
I decided to take the lot.'

'My dear Pyecraft!'

'I held my nose,' he explained.
'And then I kept on getting lighter and
lighter … and helpless, you know.

'What the goodness am I to do?'

There's one thing pretty obvious,' I said,
'that you mustn't do.
If you go out of doors you'll go up and up.'

I waved an arm upward.
'They'll have to send a plane after you
to bring you down again.'

'I suppose it will wear off?'

I shook my head.
'I don't think you can count on that.'

He kicked out at the chairs
and banged the floor.
He behaved very badly.
The things he said about me
and my grandmother!

'I never asked you to take the stuff,' I said.

I ignored the insults he was giving me,
and sat down in his armchair.
I began to talk to him
in a sober, friendly fashion.

I pointed out to him
that he had brought it upon himself.

He didn't like this,
and for a time we argued the point.

'And then,' I said,
'you wouldn't call it by its proper name.
You wouldn't call it Fat,
which is what it is,
but Weight.
You …'

'Yes, yes, yes!
I know all that!
What am I to do?'

'Well, you must adapt.
This is your new life.
You must adapt yourself to it.
You could learn to walk about
on the ceiling with your hands.'

'I can't sleep,' he said.

'That's no problem.
You could sleep underneath the mattress.
We could fasten the blankets
and sheets with tapes.
You could have a ladder,
and have all your meals
on the top of your bookcase.
Any time you wanted to get to the floor,
you could just pull out a heavy book,
and hold on, and down you'd come.'

The more I thought about it,
the more interested I became.
I am a handy sort of man with a screw-driver,
and I could see all sorts
of clever adaptations for him.
I could run a wire

bells – for servants

to bring his bells within reach.
I could turn all his electric lights up
instead of down, and so on.

The whole thing was really interesting to me.
It was delightful
to think of Pyecraft
crawling about on his ceiling

lintel – the top of the door

and clambering round the lintel
of his doors from one room to another.

And never,
never,
NEVER coming to the club any more …

Then, you know,
my cleverness got the better of me.
'By Jove, Pyecraft!' I said.
'All this is totally unnecessary.'

Before I knew what I was saying,
I blurted it out.

'Lead underwear!' I said,
and the mischief was done.

Pyecraft almost began to cry.
'I could be right ways up again,' he said.

I gave him the whole secret
before I saw where it would take me.

By Jove – an old-fashioned oath

'Sew lead discs all over your underwear
until you have enough.
Have lead-soled boots.
Carry a bag of solid lead,
and the thing is done!
Instead of being a prisoner here
you can go out again!
Pyecraft; you may travel!'

A still better idea came to me.
'You need never fear a shipwreck.
All you need do is just slip off
some of your clothes,
pick up your bag,
and float up in the air.'

'By Jove!' he said in his excitement.
'I shall be able
to come back to the club again!'

That pulled me up short

'Yes,' I said, faintly.
'Yes … of course … you will.'

He did.
He does.
There he sits behind me now,
eating a third round of buttered teacake.
No one in the whole world, except me,
knows that he weighs practically nothing.
That he is a mere mass of gas,
a cloud in clothing.
Nothing more!

There he sits watching
until I have done this writing.
Then, if he can,
he will waylay me.
He will come billowing up to me …

He will tell me over and over again
all about it –
how it feels,
how it doesn't feel,
how he sometimes hopes
it is passing off a little.

waylay – catch

billowing – he
moves like a cloud

Always somewhere he will say,
'The secret's keeping, eh?
If anyone knew
I should be so ashamed …
Makes a fellow look such a fool, you know.
Crawling about on a ceiling and all that …'

Now to get out
while avoiding Pyecraft.
He is sitting, as usual,
right between me and the door.